THE BASICS

OF THE

ELLIOTT WAVE PRINCIPLE

by Robert R. Prechter, Jr.

Published by

NEW CLASSICS LIBRARY

a division of

Post Office Box 1618, Gainesville, GA 30503 USA
800-336-1618 or 770-536-0309 or fax 770-536-2514

THE BASICS
OF THE
ELLIOTT WAVE PRINCIPLE

Printed in the United States of America

First Edition: August 1995
Second Edition: February 1996
Third Edition: April 2000
Fourth Edition: June 2004

For information, address the publishers:
New Classics Library
a division of
Elliott Wave International
Post Office Box 1618
Gainesville, Georgia 30503 USA

Cover design: Marc Benejan
Production: Pam Greenwood

ISBN: 0-932750-63-X

CONTENTS

FOREWORD

By understanding the Wave Principle, you can anticipate large and small shifts in the psychology driving *any* investment market and help yourself minimize the emotions that drive your own investment decisions. Where did this valuable tool come from?

Ralph Nelson Elliott, a corporate accountant by profession, studied price movements in the financial markets and observed that certain patterns repeat themselves. He offered proof of his discovery by making astonishingly accurate stock market forecasts. What appears random and unrelated, Elliott said, will actually trace out a recognizable pattern once you learn what to look for. Elliott called his discovery "the Wave Principle," and its implications were huge. He had identified the common link that drives the trends in human affairs, from financial markets to fashion, from politics to popular culture.

Robert Prechter resurrected the Wave Principle from near obscurity in 1976. Bob was working as an analyst for Merrill Lynch when he discovered the complete body of R.N. Elliott's work in the New York Public Library.

Mr. Prechter and A.J. Frost published *Elliott Wave Principle* in 1978. The book received enthusiastic reviews and became a Wall Street bestseller. Their forecast called for a roaring bull market in the 1980s, to be followed by a record bear market. Mr. Prechter left Merrill Lynch in 1979 to start the monthly publication, *The Elliott Wave Theorist*, and a new focus for Wall Street and investors worldwide was born.

Knowledge of the Wave Principle among private and professional investors grew dramatically in the 1980s. The stunning accuracy of the forecasts in *The Elliott Wave Theorist* earned numerous awards, and received a level of recognition that no other such publication has ever achieved.

It is no coincidence that the global acceptance of the Elliott Wave Principle has paralleled the growth of Elliott Wave International (EWI), the market analysis and publishing corporation founded by Robert R. Prechter, Jr. In the two decades since then, EWI has earned the reputation as the world's premier publisher of Elliott wave analysis and investment commentary. Tens of thousands of investors use the Wave Principle to guide their financial decisions. Tens of thousands more have bought products indirectly, through distributors and representatives. Prechter and Frost's book has now been translated into French, German, Dutch, Spanish, Swedish, Polish, Japanese, Chinese, and Russian.

Elliott Wave International is one of the world's largest providers of technical analysis. The revolution in instant data transmission has given us a perfect vehicle for around-the-clock coverage of global financial markets.

We now provide institutional and private investors with 24-hour market commentary via electronic delivery. We also provide monthly publications, hotlines and educational services that include periodic conferences, intensive workshops and tutorials, video tapes, special reports and books.

ABOUT THE AUTHOR

Founder and president of Elliott Wave International, Robert Prechter has been publishing market commentary since 1976. He began his career with the Merrill Lynch Market Analysis Department in New York. In 1984, Bob set a record in the options division of the U.S. Trading Championship with a real-money trading account. In December 1989, Financial News Network (now CNBC) named him "Guru of the Decade." Bob served for nine years on the Board of the Market Technicians Association and in 1990-1991 served as its president. During the 1990s, he expanded his firm to provide analysis for institutions on every major financial market in the world. Bob has written 13 books on finance, most notably the two-volume set, *Socionomics – The Science of History and Social Prediction*. His recent title, *Conquer the Crash — You Can Survive and Prosper in a Deflationary Crash and Depression*, was a New York Times and Wall Street Journal business bestseller. In 1999, Bob received the CSTA's first annual A.J. Frost Memorial Award for Outstanding Contribution to the Development of Technical Analysis. In 2003, Traders Library granted him its Hall of Fame award.

THE BASICS

"The Wave Principle" is Ralph Nelson Elliott's discovery that social, or crowd, behavior trends and reverses in recognizable patterns. Using stock market data for the Dow Jones Industrial Average (DJIA) as his main research tool, Elliott discovered that the ever-changing path of stock market prices reveals a structural design that in turn reflects a basic harmony found in nature. From this discovery, he developed a rational system of market analysis.

Under the Wave Principle, every market decision is both *produced by* meaningful information and *produces* meaningful information. Each transaction, while at once an *effect*, enters the fabric of the market and, by communicating transactional data to investors, joins the chain of *causes* of others' behavior. This feedback loop is governed by man's social nature, and since he *has* such a nature, the process generates forms. As the forms are repetitive, they have predictive value.

Elliott isolated thirteen "waves," or patterns of directional movement, that recur in markets and are repetitive in form, but are not necessarily repetitive in time or amplitude. He named, defined and illustrated the patterns. He then described how these structures link together to form larger versions of the same patterns, how those in turn are the building blocks for patterns of the next larger size, and so on. His descriptions constitute a set of empirically derived rules and guidelines for interpreting market action. The patterns that naturally occur under the Wave Principle are described below.

The Five-Wave Pattern

In markets, progress ultimately takes the form of five waves of a specific structure. Three of these waves, which

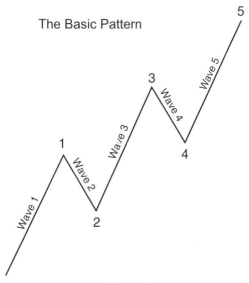

Figure 1

are labeled 1, 3 and 5, actually effect the directional movement. They are separated by two countertrend interruptions, which are labeled 2 and 4, as shown in Figure 1. The two interruptions are apparently a requisite for overall directional movement to occur.

At any time, the market may be identified as being somewhere in the basic five-wave pattern at the largest degree of trend. Because the five-wave pattern is the overriding form of market progress, all other patterns are subsumed by it.

Wave Mode

There are two modes of wave development: *motive* and *corrective*. Motive waves have a *five*-wave structure, while corrective waves have a *three*-wave structure or a variation thereof. Motive mode is employed by both the five-wave pattern of Figure 1 *and* its same-directional components, i.e., waves 1, 3 and 5. Their structures are called "motive" because they powerfully impel the market. Corrective mode is employed by all countertrend interruptions, which include waves 2 and 4 in Figure 1. Their structures are called "corrective" because they can accomplish only a partial retracement, or "correction," of the progress achieved by any preceding motive wave. Thus, the two modes are fundamentally different, both in their roles and in their construction, as will be detailed in an upcoming section.

The five-wave motive phase has subwaves denoted by numbers, and the three-wave corrective phase has subwaves are denoted by letters. Every motive wave is followed by a corrective wave. Just as wave 2 corrects wave 1 in Figure 1, the sequence A, B, C corrects the sequence 1, 2, 3, 4, 5 in Figure 2.

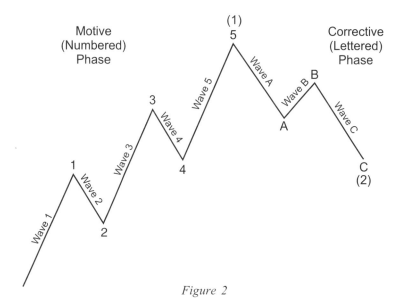

Figure 2

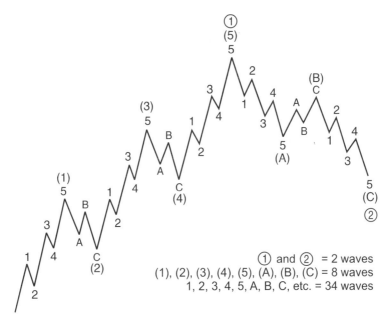

Figure 3

The Essential Design

Figure 3 not only illustrates a *larger* version of Figure 2, it also illustrates *Figure 2 itself*, in greater detail. Waves (1) and (2) in Figure 3, if examined under a "microscope," would take the same form as waves ① and ②. Regardless of degree, the form is constant. We can use Figure 3 to illustrate two waves, eight waves or thirty-four waves, depending upon the degree to which we are referring.

Now observe that within the corrective pattern illustrated as wave ② in Figure 3, waves (A) and (C), which point downward, are each composed of five waves: 1, 2, 3, 4 and 5. Similarly, wave (B), which points upward, is composed of three waves: A, B and C. This construction discloses a crucial point: Motive waves do not always point upward, and corrective waves do not always point downward. The mode of a wave is determined not by its absolute direction but primarily by its *relative* direction. Aside from four specific exceptions, which will be discussed later in this chapter, waves divide in *motive* mode (five waves) when trending in the same direction as the wave of one larger degree of which it is a part, and in *corrective* mode (three waves or a variation) when trending in the opposite direction. Waves (A) and (C) are motive, trending in the *same direction* as wave ②. Wave (B) is corrective because it corrects wave (A) and is *countertrend* to wave ②. In summary, the essential underlying tendency of the Wave Principle is that *action in the same direction as the one larger trend develops in five waves, while reaction against the one larger trend develops in three waves,* at all degrees of trend.

Nor does Figure 3 imply finality. As before, this larger cycle automatically becomes two subdivisions of the wave of *next* higher degree. As long as progress continues, the process of building to greater degrees continues. The reverse process of subdividing into lesser degrees apparently continues indefinitely as well. As far as we can determine, then, all waves both *have* and *are* component waves.

Variations on the Basic Theme

The Wave Principle would be simple to apply if the basic theme described above were the complete description of market behavior. However, the real world, fortunately or unfortunately, is not so simple. The rest of this section fills out the description of how the market behaves in reality.

Wave Degree

All waves may be categorized by relative size, or degree. Elliott discerned nine degrees of waves, from the smallest wiggle on an hourly chart to the largest wave he could assume existed from the data then available. He chose the names listed below to label these degrees, from largest to smallest:

Grand Supercycle
Supercycle
Cycle
Primary
Intermediate
Minor
Minute
Minuette
Subminuette

Cycle waves subdivide into Primary waves that subdivide into Intermediate waves that in turn subdivide into Minor and sub-Minor waves. It is important to understand that these labels refer to specifically identifiable degrees of waves. By using this nomenclature, the analyst can identify precisely the position of a wave in the overall progression of the market, much as longitude and latitude are used to identify a geographical location. To say, "the Dow Jones Industrial Average is in Minute wave ⓥ of Minor wave 1 of Intermediate wave (3) of Primary wave ⑤ of Cycle wave I of Supercycle wave (V) of the current Grand Supercycle" is to identify a specific point along the progression of market history.

When numbering and lettering waves, some scheme such as the one shown at right is recommended to differentiate the degrees of waves in the stock market's progression. We have standardized the labels as follows:

Wave Degree	5s With the Trend					3s Against the Trend		
	(↑ next is Arabic symbols)					(↑ next is caps)		
Grand Supercycle	Ⓘ	Ⓘ	Ⓘ	Ⓘ	Ⓥ	ⓐ	ⓑ	ⓒ
Supercycle	(I)	(II)	(III)	(IV)	(V)	(a)	(b)	(c)
Cycle	I	II	III	IV	V	a	b	c
Primary	①	②	③	④	⑤	Ⓐ	Ⓑ	Ⓒ
Intermediate	(1)	(2)	(3)	(4)	(5)	(A)	(B)	(C)
Minor	1	2	3	4	5	A	B	C
Minute	ⓘ	ⓘ	ⓘ	ⓘ	ⓥ	ⓐ	ⓑ	ⓒ
Minuette	(i)	(ii)	(iii)	(iv)	(v)	(a)	(b)	(c)
Subminuette	i	ii	iii	iv	v	a	b	c
	(↓ next is Arabic symbols)					(↓ next is caps)		

MOTIVE WAVES

Motive waves subdivide into *five* waves and always move in the same direction as the trend of one larger degree. They are straightforward and relatively easy to recognize and interpret. Within motive waves, wave 2 always retraces less than 100% of wave 1, and wave 4 always retraces less than 100% of wave 3. Wave 3, moreover, always travels beyond the end of wave 1. The goal of a motive wave is to make progress, and these rules of formation assure that it will.

Elliott further discovered that in price terms, wave 3 is often the longest and never the shortest among the three actionary waves (1, 3 and 5) of a motive wave. As long as wave 3 undergoes a greater percentage movement than either wave 1 or 5, this rule is satisfied. It almost always holds on an arithmetic basis as well. There are two types of motive waves: *impulse* and *diagonal triangle*.

IMPULSE

The most common motive wave is an *impulse*. In an impulse, wave 4 does not enter the territory of (i.e., "overlap") wave 1. This rule holds for all non-leveraged "cash" markets. Futures markets, with their extreme leverage, can induce short term price extremes that would not occur in cash markets. Even so, overlapping is usually confined to daily and intraday price fluctuations and even then is rare. In addition, the actionary subwaves (1, 3 and 5) of an impulse are themselves motive, and subwave 3 is specifically an impulse. Figures 2, 3 and 4 depict impulses in the 1, 3, 5, A and C wave positions.

As detailed in the preceding three paragraphs, there are only a few simple rules for interpreting impulses properly. A *rule* is so called because it governs all waves to which it applies. Typical, *yet not inevitable*, characteristics of waves are called *guidelines*. Guidelines of impulse formation, including extension, truncation, alternation,

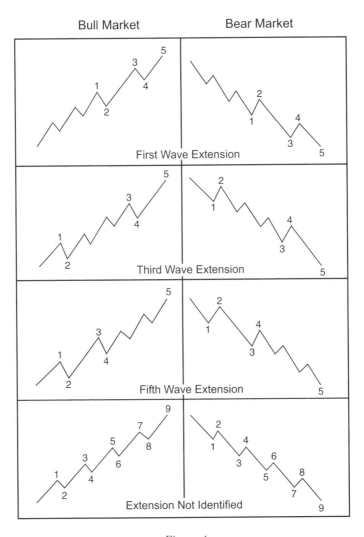

Figure 4

equality, channeling, personality and ratio relationships are discussed below. A rule should never be disregarded. In many years of practice with countless patterns, we have found but one instance above Subminuette degree when all other rules and guidelines combined to suggest that a rule was broken. Analysts who routinely break any of the rules detailed in this section are practicing some form of analysis other than that guided by the Wave Principle. These rules have great practical utility in correct counting, which we will explore further in discussing extensions.

Extension

Most impulses contain what Elliott called an extension. Extensions are elongated impulses with exaggerated subdivisions. The vast majority of impulse waves do contain an extension in one and only one of their three motive subwaves (1, 3 or 5). The diagrams in Figure 4, illustrating extensions, will clarify this point.

Often the third wave of an extended third wave is an extension, producing a profile such as shown in Figure 5.

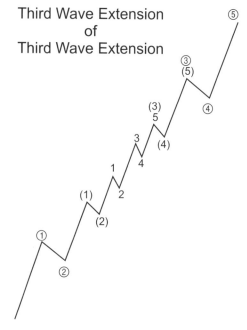

Third Wave Extension
of
Third Wave Extension

Figure 5

Truncation

Elliott used the word "failure" to describe a situation in which the fifth wave does not move beyond the end of the third. We prefer the less connotative term, "truncation," or "truncated fifth." A truncation can usually be verified by noting that the presumed fifth wave contains the necessary five subwaves, as illustrated in Figures 6 and 7. Truncation often occurs following a particularly strong third wave.

Truncation gives warning of underlying weakness or strength in the market. In application, a truncated fifth wave will often cut short an expected target. This annoyance is counterbalanced by its clear implications for persistence in the new direction of trend.

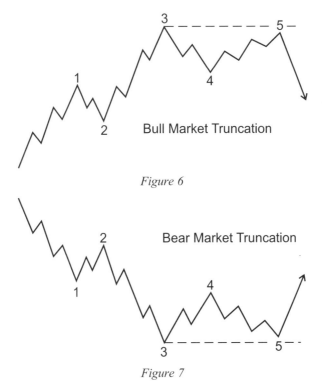

Bull Market Truncation

Figure 6

Bear Market Truncation

Figure 7

DIAGONAL TRIANGLES (WEDGES)

A diagonal triangle is a special type of wave that occurs primarily in the fifth wave position at times when the preceding move has gone "too far too fast," as Elliott put it. A diagonal triangle is a motive pattern, yet not an impulse, as it has one or two corrective characteristics. Diagonal triangles substitute for impulses at specific locations in the wave structure. They are the only five-wave structures in the direction of the main trend within which wave four almost always moves into the price territory of (i.e., overlaps) wave one. (See Figure 8.)

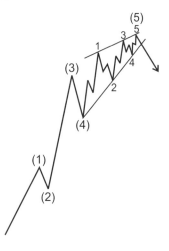

Figure 8

CORRECTIVE WAVES

Markets move *against* the trend of one greater degree only with a seeming struggle. Resistance from the larger trend appears to prevent a correction from developing a full motive structure. The struggle between the two oppositely trending degrees generally makes corrective waves less clearly identifiable than motive waves, which always flow with comparative ease in the direction of the one larger trend. As another result of the conflict between trends, corrective waves are quite a bit more varied than motive waves.

Corrective patterns fall into four main categories:

Zigzag (5-3-5; includes three types: single, double, and triple);

Flat (3-3-5; includes three types: regular, expanded, and running);

Triangle (3-3-3-3-3; four types: three of the contracting variety (ascending, descending, and symmetrical) and one of the expanding variety (reverse symmetrical);

Combination (two types: double three and triple three).

ZIGZAGS (5-3-5)

A *single zigzag* in a bull market is a simple three-wave declining pattern labeled A-B-C and subdividing 5-3-5. The top of wave B is noticeably lower than the start of wave A, as illustrated in Figures 9 and 10.

Occasionally zigzags will occur twice, or at most, three times in succession, particularly when the first zigzag falls short of a normal target. In these cases, each zigzag is separated by an intervening "three" (labeled X), producing what is called a *double zigzag* (see Figure 11) or *triple zigzag*. The zigzags are labeled W and Y (and Z, if a triple).

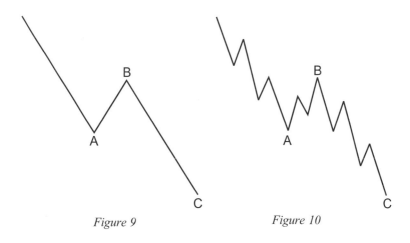

Figure 9   Figure 10

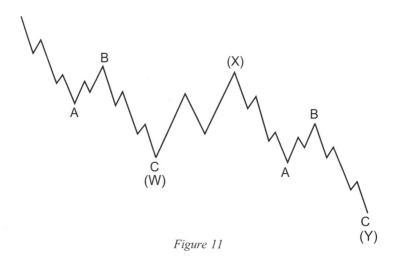

Figure 11

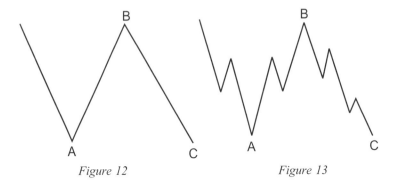

Figure 12   *Figure 13*

FLATS (3-3-5)

A flat correction differs from a zigzag in that the sub-wave sequence is 3-3-5, as shown in Figures 12 and 13. Since wave A lacks sufficient downward force to unfold into a full five waves as it does in a zigzag, the B wave reaction seems to inherit this lack of countertrend pressure and terminates near the start of wave A. Wave C, in turn, generally terminates just slightly beyond the end of wave A rather than significantly beyond as in zigzags.

Flat corrections usually retrace less of preceding impulse waves than do zigzags. They participate in periods involving a strong larger trend and thus virtually always

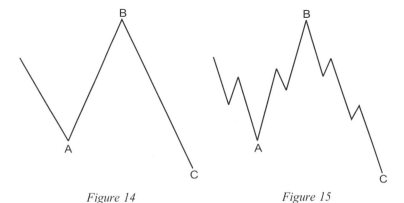

Figure 14   *Figure 15*

precede or follow extensions. The more powerful the underlying trend, the briefer the flat tends to be. Within impulses, fourth waves frequently sport flats, while second waves rarely do.

Three types of 3-3-5 corrections have been identified by differences in their overall shape. In a *regular* flat correction, wave B terminates about at the level of the beginning of wave A, and wave C terminates a slight bit past the end of wave A, as we have shown in Figures 12 and 13. Far more common, however, is the variety called an *expanded* flat, which contains a price extreme beyond that of the preceding impulse wave. In expanded flats, wave B of the 3-3-5 pattern terminates beyond the starting level of wave A, and wave C ends more substantially beyond the ending level of wave A, as shown in Figures 14 and 15.

In a rare variation on the 3-3-5 pattern, which we call a *running* flat, wave B terminates well beyond the beginning of wave A as in an expanded flat, but wave C fails to travel its full distance, falling short of the level at which wave A ended. There are hardly any examples of this type of correction in the price record.

HORIZONTAL TRIANGLES (TRIANGLES)

Triangles are overlapping five wave affairs that subdivide 3-3-3-3-3. They appear to reflect a balance of forces, causing a sideways movement that is usually associated with decreasing volume and volatility. Triangles fall into four main categories as illustrated in Figure 16. These illustrations depict the first three types as taking place within the area of preceding price action, in what may be termed *regular* triangles. However, it is quite common, particularly in contracting triangles, for wave b to exceed the start of wave a in what may be termed a *running* triangle, as shown in Figure 17.

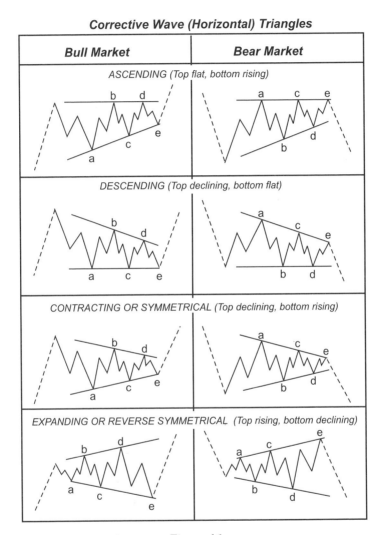

Figure 16

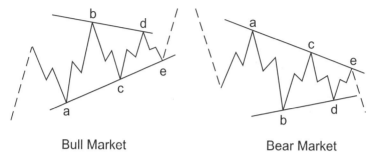

Bull Market   Bear Market

Figure 17

Although upon extremely rare occasions a second wave in an impulse appears to take the form of a triangle, triangles nearly always occur in positions *prior to* the final actionary wave in the pattern of one larger degree, i.e., as wave four in an impulse, wave B in an A-B-C, or the final wave X in a double or triple zigzag or combination (see next section).

COMBINATIONS (DOUBLE AND TRIPLE THREES)

Elliott called sideways combinations of corrective patterns "double threes" and "triple threes." While a single three is any zigzag or flat, a triangle is an allowable final component of such combinations and in this context is called a "three." A double or triple three, then, is a combination of simpler types of corrections, including the various types of zigzags, flats and triangles. Their occurrence appears to be the flat correction's way of extending sideways action. As with double and triple zigzags, each simple corrective pattern is labeled W, Y and Z. The reactionary waves, labeled X, can take the shape of any corrective pattern but are most commonly zigzags. Figures 18 and 19 show two examples of double threes.

For the most part, double threes and triple threes are horizontal in character. One reason for this trait is that

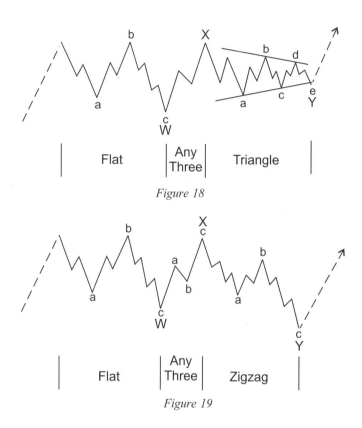

Figure 18

Figure 19

there is never more than one zigzag in a combination. Neither is there more than one triangle. Recall that triangles occurring alone precede the final movement of a larger trend. Combinations appear to recognize this character and sport triangles only as the final wave in a double or triple three.

All the patterns illustrated in this booklet take the same form whether within a larger rising or falling trend. In a falling trend, they are simply inverted.

GUIDELINES OF WAVE FORMATION

ALTERNATION

The guideline of alternation states that if wave two of an impulse is a sharp retracement, expect wave four to be a sideways correction, and vice versa. Figure 20 shows the most characteristic breakdowns of impulse waves, both up and down. Sharp corrections never include a new price extreme, i.e., one that lies beyond the orthodox end of the preceding impulse wave. They are almost always zigzags (single, double or triple); occasionally they are double threes that *begin* with a zigzag. Sideways corrections include flats, triangles, and double and triple corrections. They usually include a new price extreme, i.e., one that lies beyond the orthodox end of the preceding impulse wave.

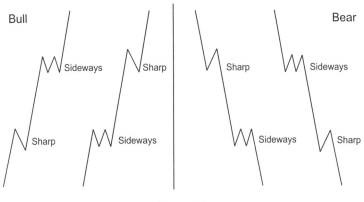

Figure 20

DEPTH OF CORRECTIVE WAVES

No market approach other than the Wave Principle gives as satisfactory an answer to the question, "How far down can a bear market be expected to go?" The primary guideline is that corrections, especially when they themselves are fourth waves, tend to register their maximum retracement within the span of travel of the previous fourth wave of one lesser degree, most commonly near the level of its terminus. Note in Figure 21, for instance, how wave 2 ends at the level of wave four of 1, and how wave 4 ends at the level of wave four of 3.

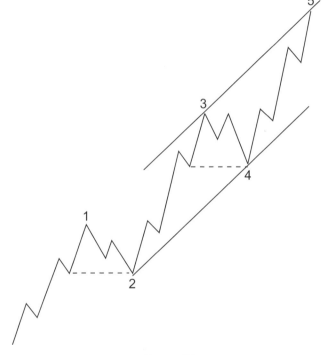

Figure 21

CHANNELING TECHNIQUE

Elliott noted that parallel trend channels typically mark the upper and lower boundaries of impulse waves, often with dramatic precision. Analysts should draw them in advance to assist in determining wave targets and to provide clues to the future development of trends.

To draw a proper channel, first connect the ends of waves two and four. If waves one and three are normal, the upper parallel most accurately forecasts the end of wave 5 when drawn touching the peak of wave three, as in Figure 21. If wave three is abnormally strong, almost vertical, then a parallel drawn from its top may be too high. Experience has shown that a parallel to the baseline that touches the top of wave one is then more useful.

The question of whether to expect a parallel channel on arithmetic or semilog (percentage) scale is still unresolved as far as developing a definite tenet on the subject. If the price development at any point does not fall neatly within two parallel lines on the scale (either arithmetic or semilog) you are using, switch to the other scale in order to observe the channel in correct perspective. To stay on top of all developments, the analyst should always use both.

Within parallel channels and the converging lines of diagonal triangles, if a fifth wave approaches its upper trendline on declining volume, it is an indication that the end of the wave will meet or fall short of it. If volume is heavy as the fifth wave approaches its upper trendline, it indicates a possible penetration of the upper line, which Elliott called "throw-over." Throw-overs also occur, with the same characteristics, in declining markets.

VOLUME

In normal fifth waves below Primary degree, volume tends to be less than in third waves. If volume in an advancing fifth wave of less than Primary degree is equal to or greater than that in the third wave, an extension of the fifth is in force. While this outcome is often to be expected anyway if the first and third waves are about equal in length, it is an excellent warning of those rare times when both a third *and* a fifth wave are extended.

At Primary degree and greater, volume tends to be higher in an advancing fifth wave merely because of the natural long term growth in the number of participants in bull markets.

LEARNING THE BASICS

The Wave Principle is unparalleled in providing an overall perspective on the position of the market most of the time. While this perspective is extremely comforting and useful, the more practical goal of any analytical method is to identify market lows suitable for entering positions on the long side and market highs offering the opportunity to take profits or enter the short side. The Elliott Wave Principle is especially well suited to these functions. Nevertheless, the Wave Principle does not provide *certainty* about any one market outcome. One must understand and accept that any approach that can identify high odds for a fairly specific outcome will produce a losing bet some of the time.

What the Wave Principle provides is an objective means of assessing the relative *probabilities* of possible future paths for the market. What's more, competent analysts applying the rules and guidelines of the Wave Principle objectively should usually agree on the *order* "of those probabilities." At any time, two or more valid wave interpretations are usually acceptable by the *rules* of the Wave Principle. The rules are highly specific and keep the number of valid alternatives to a minimum. Among the valid alternatives, the analyst will generally regard as preferred the interpretation that satisfies the largest number of *guidelines* and will accord top alternate status to the interpretation satisfying the next largest number of guidelines, and so on.

Alternate interpretations are extremely important. Your second-best "count" is an essential aspect of trading with the Wave Principle, because in the event that the market fails to follow the preferred scenario, your top alternate count becomes your backup plan.

The best approach is deductive reasoning. Knowing what Elliott rules will not allow, one can deduce that whatever remains must be the most likely course for the market. By applying all the rules of extensions, alternation, overlapping, channeling, volume and the rest, the analyst has a much more formidable arsenal than one might imagine at first glance.

Most other approaches to market analysis, whether fundamental, technical or cyclical, disallow other than arbitrarily chosen stop points, thus keeping either risk or frequency of stop-outs high. The Wave Principle, in contrast, provides a built-in objective method for placing a loss-limiting stop. Since Elliott wave analysis is based upon price patterns, a pattern identified as having been completed is either over or it isn't. If the market changes direction, the analyst has caught the turn. If the market moves beyond what the apparently completed pattern allows, the conclusion is wrong, and any funds at risk can be reclaimed immediately.

Of course, there are often times when, despite a rigorous analysis, the question may arise as to how a developing move is to be counted or perhaps classified as to degree. When there is no clearly preferred interpretation, the analyst must wait until the count resolves itself, in other words, to "sweep it under the rug until the air clears," as Hamilton Bolton suggested. Almost always, subsequent moves will clarify the status of previous waves by revealing their position in the pattern of the next higher degree. When subsequent waves clarify the picture, the probability that a turning point is at hand can suddenly and excitingly rise to nearly 100%.

The ability to *identify* junctures is remarkable enough, but the Wave Principle is the only method of analysis which also provides guidelines for *forecasting*. Many of these guidelines are specific and can occasionally yield results of stunning precision. If indeed markets are patterned, and if those patterns have a recognizable geometry, then regardless of the variations allowed, certain price and time relationships are likely to recur. In fact, real world experience shows that they do. The next section addresses some additional guidelines that are helpful in the forecasting exercise.

THE FIBONACCI SEQUENCE
AND ITS APPLICATION

Known for centuries by scientists, naturalists and mathematicians, the sequence of numbers 1, 1, 2, 3, 5, 8, 13, 21, 34, 55, 89, 144, and so on to infinity is known today as the Fibonacci sequence. The sum of any two adjacent numbers in this sequence forms the next higher number in the sequence, viz., 1 plus 1 equals 2, 1 plus 2 equals 3, 2 plus 3 equals 5, 3 plus 5 equals 8, and so on to infinity. The ratio of any two consecutive numbers in the sequence approximates 1.618, or its inverse, .618, after the first several numbers. Refer to Figure 22 for a complete ratio table interlocking all Fibonacci numbers from 1 to 144.

1.618 (or .618) is known as the Golden Ratio or Golden Mean. Nature uses the Golden Ratio in its most intimate building blocks and in its most advanced patterns, in forms as minuscule as atomic structure and DNA molecules to those as large as planetary orbits and galaxies. It is involved in such diverse phenomena as quasi crystal arrangements, planetary distances and periods, reflections of light beams on glass, the brain and nervous system, musical arrangement, and the structures of plants and animals. Science is rapidly discovering that there is indeed a basic proportional principle of nature. The stock market has the very same mathematical base as do these natural phenomena.

At every degree of stock market activity, a bull market subdivides into five waves and a bear market subdivides into three waves, giving us the 5-3 relationship that is the mathematical basis of the Elliott Wave Principle. We can generate the complete Fibonacci sequence by using Elliott's concept of the progression of the market. If we start with the simplest expression of the concept of a bear swing, we get one straight line decline. A bull swing, in its simplest form, is one straight line advance.

Fibonacci Ratio Table

NUMERATOR	1	2	3	5	8	13	21	34	55	89	144
DENOMINATOR											
1	1.00	2.00	3.00	5.00	8.00	13.00	21.00	34.00	55.00	89.00	144.00
2	.50	1.00	1.50	2.50	4.00	6.50	10.50	17.00	27.50	44.50	72.00
3	.333	.667	1.00	1.667	2.667	4.33	7.00	11.33	18.33	29.67	48.00
5	.20	.40	.60	1.00	1.60	2.60	4.20	6.80	11.00	17.80	28.80
8	.125	.25	.375	.625	1.00	1.625	2.625	4.25	6.875	11.125	18.00
13	.077	.154	.231	.385	.615	1.00	1.615	2.615	4.23	6.846	11.077
21	.0476	.0952	.1429	.238	.381	.619	1.00	1.619	2.619	4.238	6.857
34	.0294	.0588	.0882	.147	.235	.3824	.6176	1.00	1.618	2.618	4.235
55	.01818	.03636	.0545	.0909	.1455	.236	.3818	.618	1.00	1.618	2.618
89	.011236	.02247	.0337	.05618	.08989	.146	.236	.382	.618	1.00	1.618
144	.006944	.013889	.0208	.0347	.05556	.0903	.1458	.236	.382	.618	1.00

Toward perfect ratios

Figure 22

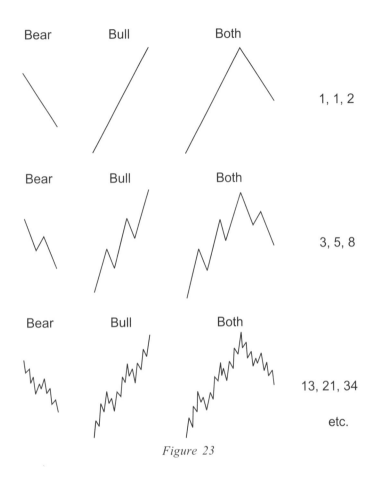

Figure 23

A complete cycle is two lines. In the next degree of complexity, the corresponding numbers are 3, 5 and 8. As illustrated in Figure 23, this sequence can be taken to infinity.

In its broadest sense, then, the Elliott Wave Principle proposes that the same law that shapes living creatures and galaxies is inherent in the spirit and attitudes of men *en masse*. The Elliott Wave Principle shows up clearly in the market because the stock market is the finest reflector of mass psychology in the world. It is a nearly perfect recording of man's social psychological states and trends, reflecting the fluctuating valuation of his own productive enterprise, and making manifest its very real patterns of progress and regress. Whether our readers accept or reject this proposition makes no great difference, as the empirical evidence is available for study and observation. Order in life? Yes. Order in the stock market? Apparently.

RATIO ANALYSIS

Ratio analysis has revealed a number of precise price relationships that occur often among waves. There are two categories of relationships: retracements and multiples.

Retracements

Fairly often, a correction retraces a Fibonacci percentage of the preceding wave. As illustrated in Figure 24, sharp corrections tend more often to retrace 61.8% or 50% of the previous wave, particularly when they occur as wave 2 of an impulse wave, wave B of a larger zigzag, or wave X in a multiple zigzag. Sideways corrections tend more often to retrace 38.2% of the previous impulse wave, particularly when they occur as wave 4, as shown in Figure 25.

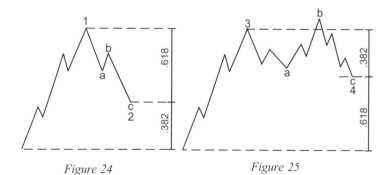

Figure 24   *Figure 25*

Retracements are where most analysts place their focus. Far more reliable, however, are relationships between *alternate* waves, or lengths unfolding in the same direction, as explained in the next section.

Motive Wave Multiples

When wave 3 is extended, waves 1 and 5 tend towards equality or a .618 relationship, as illustrated in Figure 26. Actually, all three motive waves tend to be related by Fibonacci mathematics, whether by equality, 1.618 or 2.618 (whose inverses are .618 and .382). These impulse wave relationships usually occur in *percentage* terms. For instance, wave I in the Dow Jones Industrials from 1932 to 1937 gained 371.6%, while wave III from 1942 to 1966 gained 971.7%, or 2.618 times as much.

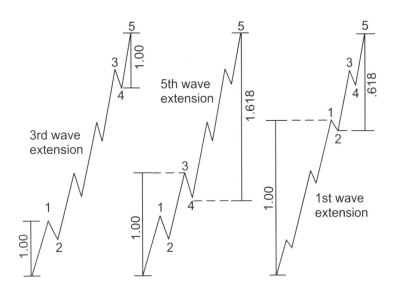

Figure 26   Figure 27   Figure 28

Wave 5's length is sometimes related by the Fibonacci ratio to the length of wave 1 through wave 3, as illustrated in Figure 27. In those rare cases when wave 1 is extended, it is wave 2 that often subdivides the entire impulse wave into the Golden Section, as shown in Figure 28.

In a related observation, unless wave 1 is extended, wave 4 often divides the price range of an impulse wave into the Golden Section. In such cases, the latter portion is .382 of the total distance when wave 5 is not extended, as shown in Figure 29, and .618 when it is, as shown in Figure 30. This guideline explains why a retracement following a fifth wave often has double resistance at the same level: the end of the preceding fourth wave and the .382 retracement point.

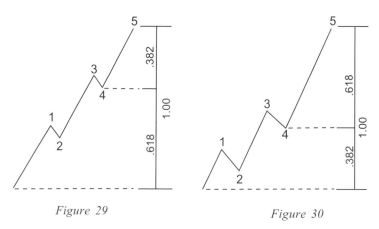

Figure 29

Figure 30

Corrective Wave Multiples

In a zigzag, the length of wave C is usually equal to that of wave A, as shown in Figure 31, although it is not uncommonly 1.618 or .618 times the length of wave A. This same relationship applies to a second zigzag relative to the first in a double zigzag pattern, as shown in Figure 32.

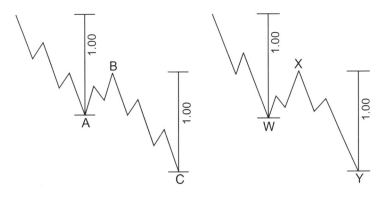

Figure 31   *Figure 32*

In a regular flat correction, waves A, B and C are, of course, approximately equal. In an expanded flat correction, wave C is usually 1.618 times the length of wave A. Often wave C will terminate beyond the end of wave A by .618 times the length of wave A. Each of these tendencies

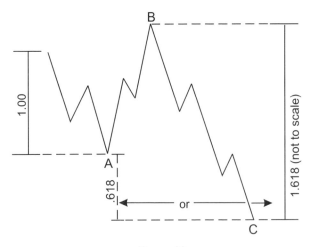

Figure 33

are illustrated in Figure 33. In rare cases, wave C is 2.618 times the length of wave A. Wave B in an expanded flat is sometimes 1.236 or 1.382 times the length of wave A.

In a triangle, we have found that at least two of the *alternate* waves are typically related to each other by .618. I.e., in a contracting, ascending or descending triangle, wave e = .618c, wave c = .618a, or wave d = .618b. In an expanding triangle, the multiple is 1.618.

In double and triple corrections, the net travel of one simple pattern is sometimes related to another by equality or, particularly if one of the threes is a triangle, by .618.

Finally, wave 4 quite commonly spans a gross or net price range that has an equality or Fibonacci relationship to its corresponding wave 2. As with impulse waves, these relationships usually occur in percentage terms.

These guidelines increase dramatically in utility when used together, as several are simultaneously applicable in almost every situation at the various degrees of trend.

PERSPECTIVE

What the Wave Principle says is that mankind's progress (of which the stock market is a popularly determined valuation) does not occur in a straight line, does not occur randomly, and does not occur cyclically. Rather, progress takes place in a "three steps forward, two steps back" fashion, a form that nature prefers. As a corollary, the Wave Principle reveals that periods of setback in fact are a requisite for social (and perhaps even individual) progress.

Until a few years ago, the idea that market movements are patterned was highly controversial, but recent scientific discoveries have established that pattern formation is a fundamental characteristic of complex systems, which include financial markets. Some such systems undergo "punctuated growth," that is, periods of growth alternating with phases of non-growth or decline, building fractally into similar patterns of increasing size. This is precisely the type of pattern identified in market movements by R.N. Elliott some sixty years ago.

Most important to individuals, portfolio managers and investment corporations is that the Wave Principle often indicates in advance the relative *magnitude* of the next period of market progress or regress. Living in harmony with those trends can make the difference between success and failure in financial affairs.

To obtain a full understanding of the Wave Principle, including the terms and patterns, please read *Elliott Wave Principle* by A.J. Frost and Robert Prechter. We wish you every success.

GLOSSARY

Alternation (guideline of) - If wave two is a sharp correction, wave four will usually be a sideways correction, and vice versa.

Apex - Intersection of the two boundary lines of a contracting triangle.

Corrective Wave - A three-wave pattern, or combination of three-wave patterns, that moves in the opposite direction of the trend of one larger degree.

Diagonal Triangle (Ending) - A wedge-shaped pattern containing overlap that occurs only in fifth or C waves. Subdivides 3-3-3-3-3.

Diagonal Triangle (Leading) - A wedge-shaped pattern containing overlap that occurs only in first or A waves. Subdivides 5-3-5-3-5.

Double Three - Combination of two simple sideways corrective patterns, labeled W and Y, separated by a corrective wave labeled X.

Double Zigzag - Combination of two zigzags, labeled W and Y, separated by a corrective wave labeled X.

Equality (guideline of) - In a five-wave sequence, when wave three is the longest, waves five and one tend to be equal in price length.

Expanded Flat - Flat correction in which wave B enters new price territory relative to the preceding impulse wave.

Failure - See Truncated Fifth.

Flat - Sideways correction labeled A-B-C. Subdivides 3-3-5.

Impulse Wave - A five-wave pattern that subdivides 5-3-5-3-5 and contains no overlap.

Motive Wave - A five-wave pattern that makes progress, i.e., any impulse or diagonal triangle.

Irregular Flat - See Expanded Flat.

One-two, one-two - The initial development in a five-wave pattern, just prior to acceleration at the center of wave three.

Overlap - The entrance by wave four into the price territory of wave one. Not permitted in impulse waves.

Previous Fourth Wave - The fourth wave within the preceding impulse wave of the same degree. Corrective patterns typically terminate in this area.

Sharp Correction - Any corrective pattern that does not contain a price extreme meeting or exceeding that of the ending level of the prior impulse wave; alternates with sideways correction.

Sideways Correction - Any corrective pattern that contains a price extreme meeting or exceeding that of the prior impulse wave; alternates with sharp correction.

Third of a Third - Powerful middle section within an impulse wave.

Thrust - Motive wave following completion of a triangle.

Triangle (contracting, ascending or descending) - Corrective pattern, subdividing 3-3-3-3-3 and labeled A-B-C-D-E. Occurs as a fourth, B, X or Y wave. Trendlines converge as pattern progresses.

Triangle (expanding) - Same as other triangles but trendlines diverge as pattern progresses.

Triple Three - Combination of three simple sideways corrective patterns labeled W, Y and Z, each separated by a corrective wave labeled X.

Triple Zigzag - Combination of three zigzags, labeled W, Y and Z, each separated by a corrective wave labeled X.

Truncated Fifth - The fifth wave in an motive pattern that fails to exceed the price extreme of the third wave.

Zigzag - Sharp correction, labeled A-B-C. Subdivides 5-3-5.

Which Markets Do *YOU* Follow?

EWI's core market forecasting services give you coverage of every major market in the world.

The Financial Forecast Service

- *The Short Term Update:* Gives you all the information you need to time short-term moves in U.S. Markets.

- *The Elliott Wave Financial Forecast:* The award-winning resource for tracking intermediate-term patterns and forecasting upcoming U.S. market price movements.

- *The Elliott Wave Theorist*
  For Information, call customer service or visit www.elliottwave.com/wave/FFSbasics

The European Financial Forecast Service

- *The European Short Term Update:* Short-term forecasts and opportunities delivered to your computer every Monday, Wednesday and Friday.

- *The European Financial Forecast:* You get monthly analysis, commentary, and forecasts of Europe's major markets over the next 30-45 days.

- *The Elliott Wave Theorist*
  For Information, call customer service or visit www.elliottwave.com/wave/EFFSbasics

The Asian-Pacific Financial Forecast Service

- *The Asian-Pacific Short Term Update:* Coverage of the near-term swings in the major Asian-Pacific stock indexes every Sunday, Tuesday and Thursday afternoon.

- *The Asian-Pacific Financial Forecast:* Timely, monthly analysis and forecasts for the major stock indexes in Japan, China, India, Australia, Singapore and Hong Kong.

- The Elliott Wave Theorist
  For Information, call customer service or visit www.elliottwave.com/wave/APFFSbasics

Futures Junctures Service

- *Daily Futures Junctures:* Provides daily opportunities to capitalize on the hottest commodities available.

- *Monthly Futures Junctures:* Details the futures markets that have the most promising patterns

- *The Elliott Wave Theorist*
  For Information, call customer service or visit www.elliottwave.com/wave/FJSbasics

Global Market Perspective

- *Global Market Perspective:* The complete resource for tracking the intermediate direction of the world's largest markets.
  For Information, call customer service or visit www.elliottwave.com/wave/GMPbasics

The Elliott Wave Theorist

Bob Prechter gives you exclusive insight on long-term Elliott wave trends so you can see how it all fits together and recognize signals in the marketplace. The Theorist comes as part of your subscription to each of the packages listed above.

For more information, email customerservice@elliottwave.com
or call 800.336.1618 or 770.536.0309 and mention code: BASICS

NEW CLASSICS LIBRARY

Elliott Wave Principle
A.J. Frost and
Robert R. Prechter, Jr.
$29

Conquer the Crash
Second Edition
Robert R. Prechter, Jr.
$29.95

The Mania Chronicles
Peter Kendall and
Robert R. Prechter, Jr.
$119

SOCIONOMICS
2 Book Set
Robert R. Prechter, Jr.
$59

View from the Top of the Grand Supercycle
Robert R. Prechter, Jr.
$29

Market Analysis for the New Millennium
edited by
Robert R. Prechter, Jr.
$39

At the Crest of the Tidal Wave
Robert R. Prechter, Jr.
$49

Prechter's Perspective
edited by
Peter Kendall
$27

R.N. Elliott's Market Letters (1938-1946)
edited by
Robert R. Prechter, Jr.
$89

The Complete Elliott Wave Writings of A. Hamilton Bolton
edited by
Robert R. Prechter, Jr.
$89

The Elliott Wave Writings of A.J. Frost and Richard Russell
edited by
Robert R. Prechter, Jr.
$89

R.N. Elliott's Masterworks
edited by
Robert R. Prechter, Jr.
$34

Beautiful Pictures From the Gallery of Phinance
Robert R. Prechter, Jr.
$39

How to Forecast Gold and Silver
Robert R. Prechter, Jr.
$179

Leonard of Pisa
Joseph and
Frances Gies
$21

www.elliottwave.com/books

EWI's Catalog of Educational Resources, Including Downloadable eBooks and Online Video Courses, Will Help You Master Elliott Waves

Streaming Online Video Courses

Titles include:
- 5 Options Strategies Every Elliott Wave Trader Should Know
- How to Trade the Highest Probability Opportunities: Price Bars and Chart Patterns
- How to Use the Wave Principle to Boost Your Forex Trading
- How to Select and Trade Individual Stocks
- How You Can Identify Turning Points Using Fibonacci
- How to Use Elliott to Improve Your Options Trading Strategies: Volatility Strategies

Browse Online Courses
http://www.elliottwave.com/wave/courses

CHOOSE FROM A LIST OF POWERFUL COURSES

Downloadable and Printable eBooks

Titles Include:
- How to Trade the Highest Probability Opportunities: Price Bars and Chart Patterns
- Trading the Line - How to Use Trendlines to Spot Reversals and Ride Trends
- How You Can Identify Turning Points Using Fibonacci
- How to Trade the Highest Probability Opportunities: Moving Averages
- How to Use Elliott to Improve Your Options Trading Strategies: Vertical Spreads

Browse eBooks
http://www.elliottwave.com/wave/ebks

CHOOSE FROM A LIST OF POWERFUL EBOOKS